TERMINAL HUMAN VELOCITY

Christina Olson

STILL
HOUSE
PRESS

FAIRFAX, VA

Stillhouse Press is an independent, student-run nonprofit press based out of Northern Virginia and established in collaboration with the Fall for the Book festival.

Library of Congress Control Number: 2016953139
ISBN: 978-0-9969816-0-6

Art Direction & Cover Design: Douglas J. Luman
Interior Design: Kady Dennell
Managing Editors: Benjamin Brezner & Melanie Tague
Cover Photo: Jerzy Durczak

TABLE OF CONTENTS

For Benjamin

TERMINAL HUMAN VELOCITY

On the night of December 2, 1979, Elvita Adams jumped from
the 86th floor of the Empire State Building—only to be blown
back onto the 85th floor and left with a broken hip.

you were on a ledge
you were looking down

you jumped
but you bungled
your calculations

> *a 29-year-old woman*
> *weight 130 pounds*

you jumped
1,050 feet high

> $F = mg$

> *in which*
> *force = mass*
> *x acceleration of gravity*
> *(assume g = 9.8 m/s/s)*

this is Newton

though a falling body
is subject to drag

so terminal velocity
of a falling human
is really more like

$$V_t = \sqrt{\frac{2mg}{\rho A C_d}}$$

> *in which*

Vt = terminal velocity
m = mass
g = acceleration due to gravity
p = density of fluid [air]
A = relative area
Cd = coefficient of drag

in New York
there are always
other forces at work

like, you are depressed,
black, from the Bronx
about to be evicted

> *plus, the wind*
> *sometimes really tall buildings*
> *make their own weather*

you should have hit
the pavement below

after 10 seconds
after falling 134 mph

but the wind that night
the wind   30 mph
the opposite direction

it caught you
you only broke
a hip

later, you said *I guess the good Lord*
didn't mean for me to die just yet

or, you know, physics
dear Elvita

    you fell only one story

you didn't need rescue

this is one story

ONE

LAST SUPPERS

In 1992, Arkansas convict Ricky Ray Rector, who had brain damage from shooting himself in the head after killing a police officer, ate a final meal of steak, fried chicken, and cherry Kool-Aid, but famously said he wanted to save his pecan pie for later.

Some request Mexican lunch, whole
bags of Jolly Ranchers, one jar
of dill pickles. Beer, though they know
they won't see it. Cigarettes
they can't smoke. More Dr Peppers
and RC Colas than Cokes. Anything
chicken-fried that can be.
And of course some say *Nothing*
or *Fuck you* or *I'll have what they're having.*
They mean the wardens. They mean the living.

Joan of Arc asked for communion.
Adolf Eichmann, Carmel wine.
Ted Bundy: nothing special.
Timothy McVeigh: two pints
ice cream, mint chocolate chip.

The most popular: cheeseburger
and fries. How many of those
have you eaten: the diner ones
under blankets of winter lettuce;
the take-out scarfed one-handed
from a bag on the turnpike;
the ones your father shaped
with bare hands and grilled
on Saturday afternoons, the whole
neighborhood smelling of char?

Some want only coffee: wired
for the wiring.

Some appreciate wholeness:
entire chickens, twelve eggs.
Some request hard-boiled

eggs and chili dogs, in pairs,
as if to board the ark
of the stomach, mated for life.

In Indiana, a man requests only fruit.
One mango. One pineapple. One coconut.
He eats the fruit with his hands
and dreams of the beach.

In Iowa, a man who killed a doctor
asks for a single, unpitted olive.

Is a meal the food on the plate
or the company one takes it with?
Is it what we taste or what we want
it to taste like? They close their eyes and will
the fried chicken to taste like their mamas',
the ice cream cone to drip on a green lawn,
the Cheez Doodles to come from a gas station
on a day when the wind smells like ocean.

What breaks your heart is the specificity:
banana pudding (with real bananas)
twelve buttered bread slices
fried chicken (cooked in garlic powder and red pepper)
four slices of cheese or one-half pound of grated cheddar cheese
chocolate birthday cake with 2/23/90 written on top and seven pink
candles

One writes *Justice, Equality, World Peace.*

The inmates count the days,
the hours, the fried shrimp
between them and their deaths.
Some of them ask to eat
in the yard. Some want
a friend, others only a window.

They killed and raped,
shot and drowned.
Their crimes are as real

as the food they dreamed.
Free people can eat
ice cream whenever they like.
They have not lost that right.
The inmates have lost the right,
but not the desire.

Anyway, you can't trust
a prison window.
The bars cut the world
into manageable worlds,
little slices.

Mitterrand, though not executed,
knew he was dying. He called
his cancer a lemon on good
days and a grapefruit
on bad. He bowed
his head under a white napkin
and ate one, two ortolan.
He ate nothing else and died
ten days later, bones
and a song in his throat.

I'm saving this pie for later.
I'm full right now.

SON OF A VOYEUR

At night, the son waits up
for his father to come in,
shoes wet from the sprinklers

in the neighbors' lawn, three
houses down—Kacy Williams,
who likes nighttime showers,

who walks from bathroom
to closet in the black mirror
of unblinded windows,

whose body two years ago
got interesting, who thinks
no one peeps in the suburbs.

That Kacy, says the voyeur,
now she's gotten interesting,
huh, & his son looks only

at the floor, the commas
of grass clippings dangling
from his father's pants cuffs.

He is young, like Kacy,
too young to do anything.
His father leaves each

weeknight at nine, prime
time on the East Coast.
The voyeur's wife, gone

these four years. The son,
who knows everything
his father's up to.

That summer, I asked
my mother what *voyeur*
meant & she said, *Someone*

who likes to watch & then met
my eyes, both hands still
on the wheel: *Wait. Why?*

We lived in Carolina then
& every day I came home
from daycare with questions:

*How come we call them roaches
but Miss Tommy calls them
palmetto bugs? What's a fag?*

Who's Jesus? Sometimes
my pockets were stuffed
with notes we were to discuss

& sign & return: *Christina
doesn't seem to know* any
of the stories of the Bible.

My father rolled his eyes
& threw them in the trash.
We were neither there

nor here. We were waiting
for a secular daycare to open,
for a better job up north,

for the days to go cool again.
Down the street lived a son
& his father, & further

down, a girl named Kacy.
One night the son waited
& then hit his father

many times with a hammer
as he screamed *You are disgusting.*
When the cops put him

in the back of the car,
the lights fell red on his face.
The father didn't get up. The son

took the money that kind
people sent & mailed it to the Williams
with a note: *Blinds.*

That summer, Culture Club's
hot hot hit was "I'll Tumble
4 Ya," but I thought the lyrics

were *Son of a voyeur,*
I'm the son of a voyeur. It played
on the radio as we drove

around Aiken, our car
windows rolled down, the sun
warm & everyone watching.

CONSIDER THE COELACANTH

Thought to be extinct for 65 million years, the coelacanth was found alive off the coast of Africa in 1938.

Listen: when fisherman in 2012
split the coelacanth's stomach,
they find a snack-size bag
of Lay's. Because the fish
is from Indonesian waters,
the chip flavor is *rasa rumput
laut*—nori. Seaweed.

One day in Africa, 1938, and all
we know of the fossil record
is called to testify in the trial
of human fallibility. One South
African scientist spent 14 years sailing
for another specimen. When one
finally surfaced, he hand-carried
his catch to East London. The cabbies
balked at the smell. Much later,
he would take his own life: cyanide.

The scientist knew the name
for such discoveries: *Lazarus taxon*,
one that keeps disappearing
from the fossil record. Here today,
gone tomorrow. Consider
the coelacanth. Naturally,
we'd think it extinct: we want
nothing so ugly, so useless as fins.

When humans run out of uncharted
places on land, we go underwater.
Our movie directors lead the way.
Or we go to space, like idiot
monkeys. When we burn up in re-entry,
they call us *heroes*. Peary, Shackleton,
Roy Chapman Andrews: better to explore

something unforgiving, like ice
or deserts, than something awful,
like the human heart. Pulled
onto land, we gulp air, dumb
as fishes. Our mouths open and close.

Poison, says the South African, and dies
by his own hand. *Poisson*,
say the French, and mean only *fish*.

PAIN JAR

I carry my pain in a glass jam jar
I keep near my lungs. I like to lie

and I say I can't feel it. Once
a month, I unscrew the lid

and count what it holds.
The new pains are hardest.

They are gizzard stones, gastroliths,
marbles. In this way, I am a dinosaur

or a red mullet fish or a sea lion.
When a new pain is let into the jar,

the old pains start to sand it down.
They are pain mentors.

I am not an Apatosaurus.
I do not drop the pain-stones

in my travels. No scientist will track
my path. The pains stay with me.

They will always live in my jar.
When they have been ground

to a fine powder, they turn to dust.
They smoke at the top. From there,

the oldest pains watch the new arrivals.
They show them how to live forever, as pain.

When I walk, the jar knocks at my heart.
It sounds like certain birds might.

COCKTAIL HOURS

When my father came home
from work, he would change
into his little red shorts
and run his six miles. After,
he would sit on the stoop
and drink a cold, cheap beer.

Other dads would loosen
their ties and pour something
brown, sip it while sorting
the day's mail. All day,
they had worked hard,
had been yelled at and signed

forms and laid off others.
Sometimes, they had to be
the ones who said, *I'm sorry.*
The X-ray isn't good.
They carried these moments
home in their shoulders

and lower backs. The alcohol
helped massage them out.
The dads I knew were not
sloppy or cruel. Later, I would
understand this as privilege, a sort
of suburban gift. We were lucky;

our fathers came straight home,
didn't linger over pitchers
and hot wings, didn't bitch
about their wives or make
eyes at women. Their bars
were their own kitchens.

Later, I would see this on the line.
After the last plates went out,
the head cook would break

out a bottle and small glasses.
We'd raise them to each other,
to meals and braises and sweat.

Or my friend, who, on the way
home from a beer run, will crack
one open once he turns down
his road. He knows this is stupid,
but it reminds him of his dead dad,
driving and drinking his way home

after a shift in southern Indiana.
And so his white-collar son checks
the rearview and brings the can
to his lips. We don't drink
like our mothers, whose work
might have been even harder,

changing diapers and bedpans,
their bodies turning against them
from the inside out, the children
responsible for that violence
growing surly in the basement
and living room. We drink

like our fathers, their quiet
ritual the thing we desire most
for ourselves and our lives.
It is the most grown-up
thing we can imagine, though
of course we should know better.

BLUE BLOODS

In the 1950s, scientists discovered that LAL (Limulus amoebocyte lysate), a clotting agent found in the [horseshoe crab]'s powder-blue blood, binds to fungi and endotoxins, coagulating into a thick gel around such invaders. The result: a simple, surefire way to detect impurities in pharmaceutical drugs and medical supplies.

In Charleston, the horseshoe crabs
are captured, folded in half, strapped
to stainless steel tables. Hours ago,
they were plucked from the beaches too north
of Hilton Head to be popular. Now needles
drain their blue blood. It's a scene from sci-fi,
a movie starring living fossils. Blue: copper,
not iron, chills their circulatory system.

Clipped to the table, crabs look like nothing
so much as army helmets. The chemical
leaked from their hard bodies will be used
to check the armed forces' supply of medicine.
The blood is drained, spun; *LAL, Limulus*
amebocyte lysate. Street value is fifteen grand
a quart. Something borrowed,
something blue. If you have ever lain

in a hospital bed, IV dangling like a thought,
the crab blood vetted that bag.
If your father died two years ago this month,
all the drugs the doctors tried were tested
with this cold blood. On ancient vacations,
you flipped all the horseshoes you could find.
Once you planted your sandy foot in one's back.
You waited for your father to yank you
but he shrugged: *Only crab ain't worth eating.*

Later, in the hospital, you brought him
blue crabs you'd boiled in Old Bay
and beer. You asked the nurses to look

away while you held the meat to his lips, wiped
your freckled hands on the bed sheets.
He died anyway. Overhead, though
you didn't know it then, the astronauts
on the International Space Station
reached for drugs made safe by horseshoes.

The living fossils will be bumped back
to the bay, released and dizzy.
They will recover fully, scuttle through silt
for another twenty million years.
We can't say the same for the astronauts,
the soldiers, the cancer kids in the ward,
your father. You. Your blood runs too red.

OPTIMISM

Certainly there are many
examples of the awful consequences
of man's ego, but my favorite
is the 1900 Galveston hurricane,
the horrifying self-assuredness of Victorians
and the unflappable certainty

in an invented forecast. Imagine watching
the great bathhouses fall into the ocean
the way you, tired, fall into bed
at the end of a long day, socks
still clinging to your ankles.
Or the sisters in St. Mary's, tying

the orphans in long strands
with clothesline around their waists;
when the water came up, the sea
merely slurped the noodle-chains
and pulled everyone into the water.
Later, men stood on the destroyed beach

and knew they could have listened
to the reports from Havana,
warned the town, dashed a telegraph.
You can always do something.
But to have such great unflappability,
such supreme self-confidence—

once I knew someone who was always
right. I envied how easily
the world cleaved to him, or how
he thought it did. While I worried,
he moved with the grace of animals
who know why the sun, water,

fish are all placed in easy reach.
Then, that animal is eaten
by a larger animal. But its last

thought is *I'm going to beat this!*
and even though you've seen
this episode before, you root

for the zebra, the baby
warthog, the gazelle bending
for a sip of cool water. The ego
of the middle food chain. The easy
stupidity of man. And the howling
storm—here it comes, listen,

you might even hear the Cuban friars
crying at you, please, get off the beach,
my god, you can save yourself.

WORDPLAY

*We passed the time with crosswords she'd thought to bring
inside/*What five letters spell apocalypse, *she asked me*

First date,
he bought me a stack
of pancakes, unfolded
the *Star Trib* & borrowed
a pen. I wondered then
why bother

with lipstick.
But I learned
to read upside down
over a plate of over-easies
& toast. We worked

our way through the *Times*
Monday, Tuesday &
Wednesday. Back then,
weekends were too hard.

Sometimes still are.
But the weeks
filled in around vowels
& bad coffee: WWII
margarine, Hawaiian
goose, father to Pierre:

oleo, nene, pere.
To copy,
the end of lemon?
Ape, ade. When Erie
came up, I told him
about the town

where I grew up, the dead
fish & smokestacks.
A great lake

minus an eye? *Ere.*
Fast Dick is *Trickle*,
former Bear Dick
is *Butkus.*

Other couples cozied
in cotton sheets
but we sought out
diners & tired waitresses,
papers filched
from crumbed
tables. At breakfast
we'd meet up with *Esai*

of *NYPD Blue*
fame. Black pen,
all caps except
for Es: big E
takes four
strokes, little
e only one. Memo

to Shortz: Caesar
more likely said
[nothing] or maybe
ahhhhhhhHHH!
as he fell, but
I'll give you your
et tu. Friends say
we look old already,
bent over smudged
pages & barely speaking.

In China, they can't
have crosswords: no
translation, no such thing
in a language
built of phonetics.
Each word a radical.
How could you

fit the lovely *teardrop*—
built of *eye* & *water*—
in any box?

Now & then we exchange,
yes, cross words,
but a hatred
for weekenders
that hide whole
phrases in single squares
brings us back

every time. There's
no way *I love you*
fits in that small
white house.
Look at it: eight
letters.
Look at all
the room it takes up
on the goddamn page.

THESE ARE THE THOUSANDS

Do the math: a set of fake mustaches
and one friend dead of heart failure. One first love,
one first dog. If I hit a dog he licks my hand

in the morning. If I hit a man I love,
he cowers like a dog. When I leave,
I take the dog. Two years in a row, someone

dies while I am on a plane. I take both
calls at the luggage carousel, pluck the wrong
black suitcase when my father cries. Two

states away, my mother is a new divorcée. One
night, three different men want my number—
some sort of record, still unbroken. Three years

in Minnesota under a snowglobe sky. Three weeks
and I know it will never be home: there's
four Indian restaurants in town and not one

decent chana masala. Every cardamom pod busted,
the seeds long gone. Instead, I keep five
tiny jars—ginger, chili, cumin, coriander, curry—

and eat the world in a yellow linoleum kitchen.
After that, there's five days in the workweek, room
for at least five bullets in a revolver. The sixth must be

for good luck. Or maybe I miscounted. In Florida,
I see seven alligators along the highway. In Wisconsin,
seven highway alligators. That's geography.

And I can't forget the eight weddings,
four of which end in divorce. Each time,
I return the shoes the next day, get my money back.

Nine years now I've kept cigarettes on ice
just in case. Nine years now I've dated men
with the same name for the same reason.

I count down the last ten years on my fingers.
Then I look at my hands: two clenched fists,
a blue-bruise heart. But now I get to start over. *One—*

LAST LOVE POEM FOR
ROY CHAPMAN ANDREWS

*Roy Chapman Andrews (1884-1960) was an American
naturalist and adventurer*

Get all these goddamn skulls
out of here. I can't stand
their empty eyes. Nor yours.

And you can take your stories:
bright nights in the *Yoshiwara*,
the geishas like caged birds.

The madam named Mother
Jesus. I don't believe one
polished word. Or when

you told me about drinking
whale milk from leaking teats,
first white man to do so.

You booked return passage
on a new ship: the *Titanic*,
then missed the boat. Or

the night you woke to find
four snakes, one per cot leg,
wrapped around your bed

in the Gobi. Viper Camp.
Tell me, Roy, which tall tale
of yours should I not believe

next? The blue man-eating tiger
who begged for its life
to be spared—and won it?

Or the son you loved, until
discovered it was your best
friend's child, then cut

from the preface, all wills?
I'm not like other women.
I'll leave before you drive

me off with your nonsense.
Before I find sand in our sheets.
Before my heart hardens

like an egg under the desert,
left alone for 65 million years.
Here goes one crack. Hear

this, Roy: I won't stick
around long enough
to hear the others.

EATING KIT KATS DURING THE LAST HURRICANE, WE DECIDE TO SPLIT UP

We ignored the best reports,
didn't flood the bathtub
with clean water. And when
the storm did shatter overhead,
we had only tiny candy bars,
pulled from the plastic head
of the pumpkin the treaters
never called for, our porch dark
and uninviting. We sat cross-legged
on the rug. The rain drowned
the frogs that used to keep us
awake. We were glad then
we had no children. We ached
for fiber, some green
and bright vegetable. But we
had only the candy. I said,
This is probably over, huh,
and you said, Please don't turn
this into some fucking movie.
I had meant only the storm.
Whoever calls rain *cleansing*
is a liar. Outside, something
cracked. It sounded like bone.

NO OTHER JOY

If you know no other in a long winter up north, know this one: a day
off work for an appointment. The lovely dark-haired doctor admits
to tanning and admires your red Chucks for what they are: canvas
impracticality, bright cardinals underfoot. At noon, light all the candles
in the apartment and play Aretha on the turntable, then light yourself
cigarette after daytime cigarette. When the snow begins to fall—movie-
flakes—pour a tumbler, raise a toast to small victories. Later go to
lunch at the type of place where the staff wears suspenders, and if
anyone were to see you and your love walking through the neon drifts,
they would think you happy.

WAITING SONG

This winter I'm learning to skate
the long pale streets by myself.
January. Alone. Or am I—
today, ten brown birds
lit up my balcony railing.
Morning coffee, puff of sparrow.
Men without teeth or ears

stop me on the street.
They whistle *honey, baby, darlin'*
through the dark doorways
in their smiles. At night,
I hear my neighbor cursing
the dog, Remy, that reminds him
of his wife. She's gone—ran away

with the circus. Left for a traveling
show of *Hair: The American
Tribal Love-Rock Musical*. Fifteen
months in Indianapolis, New York,
Tampa, Hong Kong. Back home,
he learns what I already know:

a dog can wait forever
hoping the only one it loves
will scratch key in the lock.
He wants to give Remy away.
I tell him rename him Hachikō,
that it's better to have someone
to split the wait with. And me,

now I know the difference
between all the blues and grays of sky,
in ice. The only trick to waiting
is knowing exactly what
you burn for—phone call,
first redbud. Downstairs,
they want her to come home

and fill their dishes. Me,
I'm just asking that the river
catch fire one last time.

SHACKLETON THANKS ELEPHANT ISLAND

*In 1916, twenty-two members of Ernest Shackleton's failed
Imperial Trans-Antarctic Expedition stayed on uninhabited
Elephant Island while Shackleton and five others sailed to South
Georgia Island in search of help. The men were rescued four and
a half months later.*

But not for your
namesake seals
and their lumpy faces,
the way they cry. Not
for seal steaks,
gray eighty ways.
Not for birds named
Gentoo and Chinstrap.
Not for bone
infections, snow
blindness, courtships
of madness.
Not for the first
solid land after
497 days of ice.
Before we landed
on you, we were
near dead, and after
landing: same.

Not for the hut
built of one small
boat. Not for elbowing
blizzards. Not for
Blackborow's clean
amputation, not
for the three inches
of guano and melted
snow that the men—
my men—slept in,
bodies small icebergs
on a sea

of shit. Not because
on you we thought
the War over.
Not for teaching
us that Hell is frozen.
In Hell, May is November.
And not for faces
so black with blubber
smoke that only
the eyes—wide, white
eyes—tell men apart.

PERSPECTIVE AS LEARNED FROM THE VELVET WORM OF NEW ZEALAND

Watch millions of horseshoe crabs
mating on the shores of Delaware Bay,

and a dance club starts to make sense.
The males pile on the female, the scrabble

of legs on shell. Morning light reveals
the detritus of orgies and dreams:

green eggs pocketed by seabirds, torn
bracelets, lost cocktail napkins.

Once you rented a white house
in Kitts Hummock with your wife.

Now she's left you. It would take
a plane 1400 years to gird the wide belt

of the universe's largest star. A therapist
tells you *Perspective is everything.*

All the velvet worms of New Zealand
can't bring back the dead, the ones

you miss. Still, it's a pretty shade of blue
for a creature born without eyes,

and if not meant for the worm: who?
Stand at the edge of the known universe

and debate yourself: these human problems
do not matter. Or they are the only matter.

THE POEM IS A LOVE STORY AND ALSO A LOVER AND TAKES ITS LAST LINE STRAIGHT FROM THE WIKIPEDIA ENTRY ON CARDINALS

So one day you're in the yard,
and this poem pulls up at the curb.
This poem wants to do you in the backseat
of the first car you ever owned,
which it just happens to be driving.
This poem will stick its tongue in your ear,
call you *baby*. In its backseat, you'll twist
like a white snake, aroused by the sight
of your own pale calves, when did they get
that muscle tone, you've still got it, oh yes
you do. Later, you smoke a cigarette
while this poem names all the North
American ducks it can.

   Or you're on the front porch
of your house, your fingers sucked dry
by cotton and tobacco, and here comes
this poem up the red road, holding a cigar box
guitar. It has a treasure map of Greenwood,
a dotted line to Robert Johnson's real grave
and X marks the spot. This poem knows
that real cornbread is not sweet
and a real guitar is a bloody stringed box
that just happens to make sound. Later,
this poem lists constellations as the rain
drums on the metal roof of the trailer
and you fall asleep like falling off a cliff.

   But there's pain in this poem, too:
long after the slip-sliding in the backseat
and summer nights drowsy with heat.
The years are measured in tax returns
and complimentary toothbrushes. The kids
have been put to bed. Friday night is one
cold beer after a day of wrestling schedule Cs.
Now it's dark on your mortgaged porch

and this poem is sleeping upstairs. Anyway, it
can't remember any of its old bird calls.
Damn this poem.   Damn this life.
You're at another crossroads, only this one
has nothing to do with music. Everything
is the blues now.

       But then there are more years,
and you're glad this poem came to you
all those decades ago. It's a nice life,
and anyway, what else were you expecting?
You think too much. It can't be all
spray-painted overpasses and playing
the penis game in a staff meeting. *Sometimes,*
this poem tells you, *people grow up.*
Its hands are busy in the sink, cleaning
a mandoline. You get it binoculars
for Christmas, promise that next year
this time, you'll go birding in Banff.
When this poem kisses you, you feel
something.

       But you don't make it to Canada.
This poem slinks off and finds a forest
to die in, and you're the only one who cries.
You used to like the woods, but after that,
you think all trees are bullshit. Your children
grow up and move out. You're back
in the yard but this time nothing's coming
up the road to save you. Except this.
Somewhere, a cardinal alights on a branch
and opens its throat: *cheer, cheer,*
cheer. What, what, what, what.

THE NEW QUIET

When a colony of bees smells the giant hornet approaching, it sets a trap. When the hornet trips in, the bees mob. Five hundred honeybees hum and vibrate. The temperature rises—115 degrees and the hornet dies. Or is it the carbon monoxide, the gray air, that does the hornet in?

Some bees will die, but not too many. Cost-benefit ratio analysis. Calculated sacrifice.

Last night, at a show, we watched three drunk men take off their shirts and ram the crowd. Security was useless, but you—you stepped in and shoved them back, hard. Beer-brave, I bit one on the shoulder. After the set, three people told me they were glad you were there. Don't you see? Once, we were hornets. Now we are honeybees, and we are singing.

FALLEN FROM A SUBWAY PLATFORM, YOU CHOOSE ONE OF FOUR WAYS TO SURVIVE

People trapped on the tracks have to rely on their own quick thinking. After assessing your surroundings, you should consider four options.

1.
Harness humanity. It will help
if you have been crazy-pushed
or fallen. Less if you jumped
to retrieve an iPhone. Do not
be drunk. Still: raise your voice
over the buzz of white noise.

Hold up your arms. On a good
day, many arms will meet yours.
You will be raised as if by birds,
by dolphins. Your armpits ache
for weeks. Perhaps you'll be saved

by a single hero, someone attentive
and brave. This is good too.
Now you each have an origin story.

2.
Are you thin.
Is it Manhattan.
There may be

room between
tracks and platform.
Hold your breath.

Channel that single
Pilates class. Spine
aligned. You are

a paper doll. You
are a knife's edge.
You have never

been so radiant.
The train passes
with an inch to spare.

3.
Between tracks lies the third rail. It buzzes
and hums. 660 volts. Rattlesnakes and hornets
give more warning, which is to say, any.

In 1981, chased by a mob, a man leapt onto the tracks.
He hit the rail. He flipped over. Six deep breaths,
and then he reached and touched it again. The second
touch shocked bystanders quiet.

4.
Drainage pit, wet puddle,
it doesn't matter. A few
stations have them.
There may be room.
The train groans
around a final bend.

The crowd is quiet.
The crowd is screaming.
Still, the arms do not
appear. Your life is
in your own hands,
as it always has been.

Deep breath. Face down.
You could still be open
casket. You feel the vibrations
first. Then the screaming
of brakes, the whoosh

of hell's air. If the pit

isn't deep enough,
you'll wear your ankle
skin like a halo.
Achilles at your ears.
Or perhaps you emerge
like the cicada, wet
and new, singing.

TWO

SELF-ESTEEM POEM

Don't worry about the last line,
since no one will reach it.

In the mornings, assign tasks
you really should outgrow.

Creep colleagues on the Face,
hunt for double chins in ex-lovers.

If they have new babies, say
they look like frogs. Their wives

must be hideous. And the charts:
where's your first book lurking

these days? It's outselling
Graduate Texts in Mathematics.

This is tempered by the fact
that somewhere in a state

where you read, a signed copy
is going for $9.58 + shipping.

William Logan told *Poetry*,
Don't think you're the only bastard

who ever suffered—just write
as if you were. Don't worry,

this poem won't make it
into any book, and the old song

about art can start up again
in your head. It's playing

on a jukebox at a bar across town,
the one with the dripping bathroom.

*

Once, at that bar, a roach ran up
your leg. You were brought a beer

as an apology. You took it,
as you'd accept it now.

Free always trumps jointed legs,
and anyway, pour a little

out for the insect who lives
up to a week without a head.

No head, no mouth. No mouth,
dead from thirst by day eight.

Drag your body, that sad sack
of meat and hair, to the edge

of the water, where the ocean
yawps and roars and serves

as a reminder that something
larger is always behind you.

How reassuring, you think.
You can barely swim, but no one

can in open water. We'll all
fail in our journeys, or be eaten

by sharks by end of day. Here,
you can breathe. Here, you feel

safe. You can drink all the salt
water your heart desires.

Go on, open your mouth
while you still have one.

PAST PERFECT

Already what I knew to be true
is all tenses: *has* changed, *is* changing,
will change. No more planet
Pluto. Welcome Nunavut.
I thought I heard the Spanish alphabet dumped
the long lazy roll of the *doble ele*,
and though I've since been corrected,
I liked it better when I thought it retired
to mango plantations, blue parrots screaming
overhead. Pretty soon farewell to polar bears
and the very last card catalog
and my parents—and haven't you too
wondered which of your friends will die
first and will it be anything like *The Big Chill*
and if yes, which one of you gets
to be Kevin Kline in tiny gray shorts?

It's easier to say goodbye to places
because they're what you carry with you
and after enough new driver's license photos
you actually pull a good one: nice hair,
something resembling a chin. Sometimes
I miss only stupid things: a set of blue
plates we stole three apartments ago,
the perfect shade of green they turned
under a thin coat of yolk. Their chipped
lips. Better to focus on the plates
than which one of you will die first. Envy
the television hippopotamus you watched
together on the last night in your old place.
The dry British narrator: *Their courtship
is quick. She tries not to drown.*

GREETING THE BEAR

epithalamium for myself

Dear stupid, dear server, dear evening
shadow. You are right to have waited
this long. Marriage is coming home

to a mess you didn't make. It is a bear,
drunk in the bathroom, black paws knocking
all the aerosols off the shelf. It is falling asleep

while someone explains the three-point line.
Understand that your marriage will not
save you from yourself. It will not involve camping

or staining back decks or the little lumberyard
shopping lists your fathers inked on graph paper.
Instead, you will own dogs, and clog toilets,

and once you will stay up too late to make
farting noises. The next day your mouths
will ache. You will have bad dreams

but good mornings. Mostly, your days
are mundane. Occasionally you notice
a red bird outside the window. Tuesdays

you meet downtown for gyros. In another life,
you might have been truly unfortunate: a gong
farmer, an herb strewer, a professional mourner.

When you find the mess on the stove,
the one you didn't make, set your briefcase
by the fridge and clean it up without a word.

Do this because you still remember
what it was like to be fourteen, watching
your mother slam a sponge around,

cursing loudly. This scares you. Your whole life,
it seems, has been laced with anxiety, not enough
tulips. But you will rise in the morning.

You will greet the bear. You will note the rings
around his eyes. He is searching for something
he cannot grasp. Your own paws are the right size.

SOMEBODY'S GRANDMOTHER

handed me a packet of tissues when I broke
down in the Atlanta airport after signing a lease
on a house we'd never walked through, one filled
with fleas. And somebody's grandmother
sat next to me on that long flight home, told me
that some things—her sister dying of cancer—
were worth crying over and some were just shitty,
and being grown-up means being able to tell the two apart.
Then she ordered me a ginger ale. And later that day,
I tried to pay it back. I sat next to somebody's grandmother
on her first flight in twenty years: *it is so different now,*
she kept saying. I took her elbow, showed her where
the bags would fall out. And it was somebody's grandmother
that sirens wailed for last night, then went silent at the last
light before the hospital. I used to stand under the helicopters
that cut their way across our corner of Michigan and be glad
that somebody was having a worse day than I, but now I know
that each Medevac was actually a white hummingbird,
deeply engaged in the frantic beating back of death,
and now I wish I could still see them, those little birds
full of somebody's grandmothers, those races
against the inevitability that awaits us all.

POEM FOR THE NEW YEAR

Rosé waiting in the fridge and black
eye nearly evolved, just a smudge
of yellow on my cheek. Another
year is drawing itself to a close,

having retrieved its coat and nearly
departed, pausing now in the doorway
before it steps in new snow. According to the
letters that fill my mailbox, life goes on:

graduation, wedding, mortgage.
A friend may no longer love her husband.
Another has a new dog. We are married.
And Georgia claims us now, happily.

Sometimes at dawn, or after
long runs that end downhill,
a moment of exquisite clarity:
We are all going to die. But before that

we are all going to be okay. And then
it slips away and I am left
with only coffee to make
or dull shins to ice. Living by water,

you know exactly how little
you matter. In all that blue your pink
chest disappears. But tonight
the world will gather in small rooms,

or large ones blazing with light,
or start a fire. Tonight the corks
will be carried off in the mouths
of dogs, happy to chew, while their owners

drink straight from bottles. My cheek
barely aches: now just another story
to tell over a full glass. How lucky
we all are. How exquisite this meaningless.

THE MEN I LOVE

The men I love are collecting suicide songs again, taking notes on the Golden Gate Bridge—*after a fall of approximately four seconds, jumpers hit the water at 75 miles per hour*—and playing Jeff Buckley in an empty dining room.

The men I love are crying and breaking glasses while they do the dishes, up to their elbows in apple soap and shards. The men I love are pretending to read the sports section, but their cigarette hands are trembling.

The men I love are lying in the bathtub with their arms folded and Linda Ronstadt on the AM radio, a bottle of whiskey next to the shampoo. They are cutting the seatbelts out of their Pontiacs and driving around the city, taking sharp turns.

They are leaving me clues, dropping breadcrumbs in a dark forest. This is how they show they love me. We all die; the scare is in the how.

They love me so hard. They are baking me a red velvet cake studded with California buckeyes. One leaves six white lilies and a loaded handgun on my bedside table. There is a note tied with kitchen twine to the trigger: *Make it sing.*

MARCH AGAIN

I dream of latitude, longitude:
same old song. The neighbors
finally refurl Christmas
lights. Their Santa lies
gunshot-flat amid snowdrops.

If you were two people I could
not love you more.

March incantation: ramp,
shad roe. Asparagus.
At markets the green elbows
the root vegetables back
to their burlap blankets.

In our house, the mice
run in the ceiling. And
in class, Ray Carver's
come back from the dead.
Cigarettes and dirt in his hair.
Seems we've all forgotten
the laws of mechanics.

I think that I love you
the way I love March.
Which is to say, sometimes
I get mad and throw
blue dishes. Other times,
I give mud kisses.
Which is to say,
I cheer when the lawn
pulls back its petticoats
of snow, but despair
at the piles of shit.

What I mean to say
is that I love you.
I love March. But even

as it arrives I am already
leaping ahead, wanting
the deep red of first tulip
and sunburn. Which is to say
you are here, right here,
and I can't be bothered
to be grateful.

And yet. I wake now
at first light—because light
is here again. And I hear
the first birds. And my first
thought is *Thank God.*

DEAR MONDAY

found poem composed of lines from e-mails sent from 2007-2011

Dear Monday, we are getting divorced. I hope
this Halloween nobody tells you how big
your boobs are, and I hope you get really loaded
and say the word *fuck* to a bunch of trick or treaters.
In the hallway, I passed some kid complaining
about his roommate not doing the dishes and he said
I was like, I have to do both the wash
and the dry? What am I, a single mom?

I find myself dizzy a lot these days.
It's really weird, like I'm walking around
sort of drunk even though I'm sober.
It's just the feeling of being so tired
and then feeling like there is no foreseeable time
when I will not be so tired.
I don't think we'll ever be adults.

So it goes, weird spring, with your sunny weather
and frigid temperatures and people dying
all the time. Oh my god, it just keeps snowing
and snowing and snowing. Most of the time
February makes me want to kill myself.
Twice over. That's all. It's hard,
and I don't like it. But think about June,
with so many fresh tomatoes
we'll bleed tiny white seeds
if we cut ourselves. How can I worry,
when that is all that matters?

I wish there was a training class for me
each time I went through a life adjustment:
This is how to stop crying,
this is how to stop spending all of your money,
this is how to make your favorite drinks more alcoholic.
Or, if you need to laugh at something,
then think about that image in my head

I keep having on being absent and putting
a sandwich on the table and saying,
This is your sub, see you Monday.
If we're ever adults, I'll hate us.

When I went to church on Sunday, I saw a book
entitled *The Living Bible* propped up on the table
in the vestibule. What astonished me
was the subtitle, in neat little print:
paraphrased. You know, I think
a lot of the Bible loses its power
when you start paraphrasing. Jesus
and some dudes hanging out on a beach
just doesn't really do much for me.

I tried to get happy, I really did.
I took the dog to the park and he rolled
in geese shit. Now my brain
feels as though it is pulsing like in cartoons
where brains are huge and usually evil.
Then the squirrels got into the garbage
while it was sitting on the curb and rolled
the container into the street and a truck
drove it over. In conclusion,
I think I've earned a new pair of shoes.

PUNK ROCK POEM GROWS UP

Punk rock poem moves out
of the Minneapolis co-op,
leaving seven roommates

and a wall punctuated by fists.
Punk rock poem pays down
a certified used Accord.

Punk rock poem says
it's still punk rock, it just
got a haircut. Punk rock poem

comes over with a cassoulet,
a couple of Netflix. Hey,
says punk rock poem,

remember sleeping on the roof?
Remember the night we set
all those tables on fire?

Remember Jay and throwing
full beers at the empty
moon? Punk rock poem

wants you to remember.
Punk rock poem is sure
it used to stand for something.

You can't bear to tell
punk rock poem that a basement
full of underage drunk kids

is not something. Don't you
get it, punk rock poem,
you think, *this* is the hard

business of living: the real
punk act of waking
each morning, every morning.

ON TURNING THIRTY

Once again I am the girl at the party
shouting that it would be *just so awesome*
if instead of bike lanes, cities put in

elephant lanes, waving my arms and sloshing
wine onto the woman next to me. Who am I
anyway, and why do I always come out

on these pleasant early summer evenings
as the sun is settling over the river?
Why do I always keep one lazy eye

on the wine supply, sure that the eight
bottles won't be enough, and why do I shift
awkwardly from foot to foot in shoes

I am sure everyone secretly hates? I thought
I would leave this version of me
back at junior prom, when I was blue taffeta

and taller than my date, who tasted
like orange Crush when we kissed twice
at Niagara Falls, but no, here I still am,

only with marginally better hair. Adults
tell high schoolers that the pretty girls
won't be so important one day, but that is a lie,

because since then I have worked in cubes
next to shampoo models, the type of women
who make or break the office happy-hour,

since the account managers won't go
unless they do, and then they all order
light beers while I belly up to the bar

and order whisky, neat, the way my uncles
taught me to, which I drink too quickly

and by myself. I don't like to throw parties

because I hate that I'll be there. Thirteen
years ago, had you asked me, I was pretty
sure I would have matching Tupperware

instead of repurposed margarine containers,
and that I would obey alarm clocks
and be able to touch people on the arm

without seeming like a real creep. Instead,
I'm the girl in the corner writing a poem
on the back of her coat check ticket

and wishing she hadn't accidentally worn
her father's deodorant. Maybe I'll ask
a boy to dance after all. Maybe he'll be totally

tricked into saying yes, since I smell
just like him. Maybe later we'll drive up
the only hill in town and smoke a cigarette

while we watch the sun come up, and my life
will start all over again. I'll wake up
to find that everyone loves these shoes,

that my elephant joke killed, that the wine
rinses out with vodka, and I'll stand
quietly in the very center of the room,

wearing all my mistakes
in a fine crown, having been
unanimously voted your queen.

THE ASTRONAUT FALLS IN LOVE

My brother doesn't call me
on Sundays because he Skypes

with his boyfriend, the doctor
practicing in Hong Kong.

They videochat while the moon
glows upside-down in Victoria

Harbour and it's sunny-side up
again in Atlanta. They met

because my brother, the mechanical
engineer, went to China to oversee

the production of baby strollers,
glued together with yellow dust

and sweat for thirty-one
cents an hour in Dongguan,

slapped into a shipping crate
to be sold here. I knew things

were serious when they sent
each other the links to Google Map

street views of their childhood
homes: Buffalo and its drifts,

Brisbane and its bougainvillea.
Max is Australian by way

of China, which would complicate
things with Immigration except

they can't marry anyway. My brother
sends me a video of Max he shot

with an iPhone in Starbucks. I know
this is not quite the Springsteen

*comeonbabyjumponmybike
andwe'llhitthehighway* love story

my father imagined for his only son,
but it's close enough. Like all first

romances—the kinds that unfold
in gin joints, whiskey bars and on vinyl

front seats and beach blankets
and over the very last tofu-bulgur

patty at the vegan potluck—
this one is laced with hormones

and great hope. When I ask what they
talk about, my brother says,

simply, *Everything*. And I know
what he means, because I too

used to spend the night sleeping
in the Cape Cod of a boy's arm,

a ship snug in its harbor. This is
what form love always finds first.

We fumble through minutiae
before we can work our way

up to the big stuff. Years from now,
after humans have colonized Mars,

an astronaut sleeps weightlessly
in his apartment on the four-hundredth

floor of an arboretum high rise.
He spends the red nights curled

up against his first boyfriend,
and in those heady first nights

one astronaut breathes *Are you awake*
and the atoms will stir just so

and the other crackles back
in the dark *Yes, yes*   *I'm still here.*

IN THE CROWD

You used to sit in your father's
guitar case and pretend the capo
was a baroque alligator, made it go

chomp, chomp. Then you married
someone who also loves music
except he also does not understand

how it works. Three years of teaching
himself guitar, he's got the first
twank-twank of "Heart of Gold"

down: *I want to live, I want to give.*
Instead you worship at the Church
of the Medium-Sized Venue,

and you put on closed-toe shoes
and you wrap hands around the sweaty
necks of bottles. You do not wear

ear plugs, even though you are old
enough now to know better.
You stand close, unless the crowd

is a little drunk and angry
and buzzes like bees. You help
escort out the kid who cannot

stop puking. You ask the little girls
in their adorbs blouses to put
down their phones. You might

have said, once, that if someone
did not stop talking you would
fucking kill them, and you meant it,

because that winter in Michigan
had been rough and that person
stepped in your something holy.

You will not fetishize the bassist.
You no longer want to kiss the drummer
in the dark corner, the floor

sticky under your shoes. You don't
want the set list, the flipped pick.
In the crowd, there is only

the *lub-thub* of your own heart,
keeping time. There, it slows
and you hear the voice you tune

out most days, the one that says, You,
you are going to be just fine.
You want to live, you want to give.

SELF-PORTRAIT AS THE RED BEE, WIDELY CONSIDERED ONE OF THE DUMBEST SUPERHEROES EVER CREATED

The Red Bee's secret identity is Rick Raleigh, assistant district attorney.... His superhero modus operandi is to put on a red and yellow costume and, with his trained bees and "stinger gun," fight Nazis and gangsters. His favorite bee is named Michael and lives inside his belt buckle for use in special circumstances.

1.
No one is allergic
to the allure of becoming
something else. Even
something as dumb
as a bee-trainer.

2.
For *assistant public defender,*
read *assistant professor.* For
trained bees, read *that summer*
when you tried to excise all the bad
parts of yourself that you had ever
been in thirty years of living.

3.
Right: a favorite bee.
That is not a symbol.
Even though I love bees.
Even though I am always
writing about the honeybee
thermal defense and how
it is a metaphor for that time
we went to see Lucero
and we hummed along
and I bit that drunk guy.

4.
Red like wine. Like blood.
Like I put my hand through

the glass door. It was January
and I couldn't feel a thing.
The emergency room nurse
asked me if you'd done
anything to me. *I'm the abusive
one,* I told her. She shrugged,
sewed up my finger with a fine
curved needle. It stung a little.

5.
That summer in Vermont,
I decided I would become
my very own superhero.
The bad stuff? All behind me.
I was going to be different
by the time I came home,
by the time we moved south.

I kissed you goodbye,
asked you to be strong,
wait while I was away.

No more drinking wine
late into the night in the kitchen,
no more cleaning up spills
on the tile the next day.
No more Rorschach in the red
stains. Instead, I went north,

and I remembered the person
who used to live inside of me,
and I let her out. I jumped
into rivers with Canadians
and one night, I held
a Glock and understood
the drunk allure of a handgun.

6.
If they ever made a movie
about the summer I was the
Red Bee, it would hemorrhage

money immediately. Reviews
would say: *Indulgent.*
Sentimental. Motivations unclear.
Still, when it ran on cable,
we'd watch it on Saturdays.

7.
The Red Bee had Michael.
I had you. They say if you love
something, keep it hidden
in your belt buckle, then set
it loose on your enemies.
If it doesn't come back,
it was never yours to throw
at Nazis in the first place.

8.
Did I come home
any different? I cried a lot.
Something had changed.
I mourned for the mink
I'd never again see fishing
in the river, for the artist
who came to lunch
every day with white paint
handprints on his jumpsuit.
From across the river,
they looked like doves
nipping at his hips.

9.
The Red Bee and I
are older and wiser. You
and I are older and wiser.

The Red Bee is dead
now. You and I will
be dead one day.

Still, the human race

believes in heroes. Better:
we believe we can change,
and then we do. Mostly.

10.
Do it for love of country,
for love of a good man,
for love of something
besides your stupid self.
We can be heroes. We can
buzz ourselves better. Now
when I sit next to you,
I vibrate because I am trying.

LAST LOVE LETTER FOR AUTUMN

In 2007, a Vanity Fair *editor spent months tracking down the
location of the Windows desktop image* Autumn.

A quiet lane. A sentry of sugar
maples wearing hunter orange.

The perfect, weathered barn.
Had he asked me, I could

have told him: it's nice two
weeks a year. Then comes

the raking. Palms red, weeping
blisters. Once, I thought

I loved a man in Vermont.
We had white sweaters.

We drove Route 9 and ate
butterbrickle. At the north lake

where the monster lives,
that pretty college town,

we almost convinced ourselves
our lives would matter.

And now I'll never have
to say *leaf-peeper* again,

or pretend to like the grit
of buckwheat. No more

lunches of slick orange soup.
Down here, ladies dress up

for football. The men don
belts embossed with dogs

and eagles and tigers. Pumpkins
slump in eighty degree heat.

Trick-or-treating on a beach.
You can get used to anything.

On the way back from the coast,
I see the fields have erupted

in cotton. When I squint,
it almost looks like snow.

BONAVENTURE

Savannah, Georgia

Christmas and the mercury
read eighty. We went to—
where else?—the cemetery,
that famous one. Some graves
had trees, strung with lights
that the sun winked off and on.

The soldier headstones
stood in a line. Teeth
and Spanish moss.
Some things endure.

A couple my parents' age
were on a date. He joked
and she laughed. The sound
rang wrong. On one bench,
another couple poured
martinis from a Thermos.
Everyone was in fine spirits.

The tour bus crawled
the grounds tortoise-slow.
Tourists leaned out open
windows to take it all in.
The river hummed like
a heart in a dark room.

A girl in lipstick
and Crawford-rolled hair
placed cairns on graves.
Her selection process,
she kept to herself.

The live oaks arched overhead
were planted for the king,
reserved for his navy. We walked,
our tibias not yet splinters.

Under our feet, many tibias
belonging to the many dead
were shrinking, like ice
in a cocktail on an afternoon.
This is how bone breaks down.

I have not yet mentioned
the birds and their screams.

GEORGIA, APRIL

The fire ants tunnel
under our mailbox.
Theirs is a lonely industry.

And the azaleas turn
freckled under the sun,
like college girls. Some

will last into May. Me,
I plant a garden.
I am somebody's wife.

I wear plaid a lot
because it's a uniform,
it is a purpose.

In the mornings,
they burn the fields
outside of town.

Smoke and cotton.
Peanuts and kale.
Harvest food and ash.

Sometimes it's not
so much a sunrise

as it is the sky
just goes light.

NOMENCLATURE

Two months after we married
and I didn't change my name,
you landed in the hospital
in a small Georgia town
thirty-five miles from our
small Georgia town.
The procedure was to be
routine. Instead, they
called me at work.
Frantic, I asked neighbors
to let out the dog, packed
a book and a pair of socks,
found my wedding ring
in a dish by the sink.
I brought our license,
the real one with the ink
signature. Speeding past
young cotton and burning
fields, I chanted something
like prayer: please don't die
in Reidsville, good God,
don't die in Tattnall County.
The town was a hospital
and a prison. No security
desk, nowhere to sign in.
I was left to wander,
peeking into cool rooms
that breathed for the dying
men that laid within them,
the fat blue blinds shut
to the oppressive July.
You were behind door three.
The nurses and orderlies
called me *ma'am* and *Mrs.
Dreeve-low, Mrs. Drebalow,
Mrs. Dreb-blow.* No matter
how many times I stressed
the hard V of *Drev, it's*

*Drev*low, they wouldn't get
it right. Somewhere around
the corner of that last
century, your ancestors
amputated their last syllable
and made something new.
They were German, tanned
and adrift in eastern France.
Later, they would board
big boats for Wisconsin.
Later, we would learn that
my great-grandfather met
his love in the same timber
town where you grew up.
His name was Olsen, but
there were already too many
Norwegians in upper Michigan,
and so he painted his mailbox,
made it Swedish: Olson.
This is evolution. This is
nomenclature. This is a story.
He's fine, Mrs. Dreevalow,
they said, it's nothing,
just an observation. The name
they gave us in that room
was new, it was wholly ours
and it hung in the artic
air of Room 3. In this way,
I came to understand marriage.

THREE-MONTH ANNIVERSARY

there's nothing in the etiquette guides
for a marriage   so short
so I wake early on a Saturday,
bring home Subway   the egg whites
because I want you to live forever

or at least outlast me

friends keep asking if it feels different
and they don't like the answer
no,   *not really*   *pretty much*
the same   but what did they think

bliss   *such bliss*   *seriously*
I got fired because I couldn't focus
on anything   *but the sheer bliss*

every sneeze starts as a gasp
then settles itself down

and really, there are nice little moments
like we picked all the mulberries
our hands murderous with blue juice

even the bush knows
how to be beautiful three weeks a year

PAIN JAR, AGAIN

Finally, I took my pain
jar out to the field.

They say here is where
animals come out.

I shook the stones, counted
as they did not fall.

One, two, four,
six, ten. Thirty.

From the mouth
frothed a white smoke.

A moose fringed
the edge of the forest.

The jar feels lighter
these days.

Not empty.
But—lighter.

THE USER'S GUIDE TO SYMBOLISM IN ALL MY POEMS

Alcohol is shorthand for *anxiety*, for
release. Christina dreams of pharmacies,
white coats. Her first job was in a pharmacy.

In slow hours, she lined up the bottles
by name. They rattled like bones. *Roy
Chapman Andrews*, American naturalist,

is a father figure. He appears often
to mediate issues between Christina
and her father. See: *Deus ex machina.*

A *cardinal (male)* has a crest that reminds
her of her husband's. Seven years ago,
she helped him pilot the clippers

around the globe of his skull, saw
the scars from when he fell through
the hayloft, the boards rotting underfoot.

Beast of Baluchistan (Paraceratherium)
was the largest mammal that ever lived.
Stand-in for self-esteem issues; hornless

giant rhino. Knew to ask for forgiveness,
not permission. *Beer* is the best manifestation
of flowers in a vase, of hops and hay

and all the lakes and rivers she's ever
seen. *Bourbon* is the South, where Christina
lives now. *Dark* appears often. It means

dark. *Deus ex machina* is never utilized
in Christina's poems. *Ernest Shackleton*
stands in for snowblindness. In a nightmare,

Christina wakes to only white. No shadows
to clear from her eyes. In another, she is in

a field in December with a knife. She cuts

her own hand just to understand color.
Gin tastes like 442 Brookview Drive,
and like summer, and like rosemary

when an ocean breeze carries the scent
of the hillside tangled with juniper.
Also: Christmas. *Gin* is like *gun*

only with an eye. *Horseshoe crab*
is a blue-blooded arthropod that has
and will outlive Christina, commonly

employed as bait and fertilizer. The *locust*
is both tree and insect. One turns bloody
orange in the autumn. One burrows

underground and emerges, singing,
every seventeen years. *Norway* is the ancestral
home that Christina claims. Even though

she is 1/16th Norwegian, even though
she has never stood in the cold light
of the fridge at midnight and eaten herring

in sour cream from the jar, as the men
in her family often do. *Rosemary* tastes
better than herring. It was also draped

around the Greek goddess Aphrodite
when she rose from the sea, born
of Uranus's semen, which was news

to Christina. *Singing (verb)* is totally
overused. *Terminal human velocity*
is when air acts like water, the moment

in free fall in which an object ceases
to accelerate. From a distance, a body
is just a star, bright and falling fast.

TERMINAL HUMAN VELOCITY

On the night of December 2, 1979, Elvita Adams jumped from
the 86th floor of the Empire State Building—to be blown back
onto the 85th floor and left with only a broken hip.

All day I typed the same letter
and never managed to say anything.

Instead I walked downtown and sang
to everyone I passed: *Goodbye, goodbye.*

I climbed the stairs to the twenty-ninth
floor. I was nearly thirty that winter,

I owed myself the chance to think
a last time. The first flights were easy.

In the middle I paused, remembered
a pink cake on the eleventh. Lit

a cigarette with orange flame
on the fifteenth, in honor of a lifetime

of bad decisions. But it took an hour
to get from twenty-seven

to twenty-eight. At twenty-nine
I got off, took the elevator past years

I wouldn't have and didn't want.
On eighty-six, I saw the snow was falling

up, so slightly. The window sighed
open.   I stepped.

My stomach rose in my throat, a bright
parachute. I opened my mouth

and it unraveled past my teeth
and rose faster than snow,

than sound, faster than the small
noise I thought to make.

It caught me before the first
breath fell.   I landed.

There were stars in my hip
and stars in the sky. The spire pointed

them out. I lay on my back
with my mouth open and the parachute

settled back into its pack of my body
and I counted which stars said *Hello, hello.*

NOTES

The epigraph for "Word Play" is from the song "The Temptation of Adam" by Josh Ritter.

The epigraph for "Terminal Human Velocity" ["All day long …"] is from Wikipedia.

The epigraph for "The Living Statue Speaks" takes information from *ifopa.org*.

The epigraphs for "Last Supper" and "Fallen from a Subway Platform …" borrow information from articles at *Slate*.

The epigraph for "Blue Bloods" is taken from an article in *Wired* magazine.

The epigraph for "Self-Portrait As The Red Bee" is from *http://dc.wikia. com/wiki/Richard_Raleigh*.

All italicized lines in "Last Supper" are Texas death row inmates' final meal requests, taken from *http://web.archive.org/web/20031202214318/ www.tdcj.state.tx.us/stat/finalmeals.htm*.

ACKNOWLEDGEMENTS

The author is grateful to the following publications, in which several poems in this collection originally appeared, sometimes in slightly different forms:

Anti-	"These Are the Thousands"
Atticus Review	"Somebody's Grandmother"
Birdfeast	"Optimism"
Cutbank	"Eating Kit Kats During the Last Hurricane, We Decide to Split Up"
The Fiddleback	"Son of a Voyeur"
Gargoyle	"On Turning Thirty"
H-ngm-n	"Waiting Song"
Hobart	"Last Suppers"
The Ledge	"Wordplay"
	"March, Again"
Linebreak	"Past Perfect"
The Nassau Review	"The New Quiet"
The Nervous Breakdown	"The Astronaut Falls in Love"
Paper Darts	"The Poem is a Love Story and Also a Lover and Takes Its Last Line Straight from the Wikipedia Entry on Cardinals"
	"Perspective As Learned from the Velvet Worm of New Zealand"
Rhino	"Punk Rock Poem Grows Up"
River Styx	"Blue Bloods"
Salamander	"Three Month Anniversary"
Silk Road Review	"Fallen From a Subway Platform, You Choose One of Four Ways to Survive"
Sou'wester	"Terminal Human Velocity"
	["All day long …"] (as "The Jump")
Water~Stone Review	"The Men I Love"
Willow Springs	"Shackleton Thanks Elephant Island"

"No Other Joy" is anthologized in *The Best Creative Nonfiction, Volume Three* (W. W. Norton, 2009).

"Dear Monday" is anthologized in *Writing That Risks* (Red Bridge Press, 2013).

"Last Love Letter for Autumn" is anthologized in *Stone, River, Sky: An Anthology of Georgia Poems* (Negative Capability Press, 2015).

Some of these poems also appear in the chapbook *Weird Science* (Paper Nautilus, 2016).

AUTHOR'S THANKS

This book exists because of favors, fellowship, and friendship, and for that reason, the following deserve extra big shout-outs.

Thanks to the folks of Poet's Choice, and especially to W. Todd Kaneko for inviting me to join so many years ago. Thanks to my writer colleagues first at Grand Valley State University, and now at Georgia Southern University. Before there were those schools, there was Minnesota State University.

I am grateful for the careful eyes and forces that are Marcos L. Martinez, Benjamin Brezner, Melanie Tague, Douglas Luman, Michelle Weber, and Meghan McNamara at Stillhouse Press. I am thankful for the Vermont Studio Center and the fellowship that permitted me to finish and finalize this book.

Thanks to Aimee Nezhukumatathil, Richard Robbins, and Richard Terrill for their many years of guidance. Thank you to Keetje Kuipers and Matthew G. Frank. Thank you to Michael Chouinard, Brian and Janine Dunleavy, Chad Kuyper, Al Martinez, Stacie McDaniel, Laura Moore, Jean Prokott, Jennifer Ronsman, Jared Sexton, Amanda Schumacher, Darren Wieland, Elizabeth Willingham, Amy and Nick Zieziula, and you, because I am forgetting you.

Thanks to my family, and thanks for all those conversations about Shackleton.

And biggest thanks to Benjamin Drevlow, for everything. But only everything.

This book would not have been possible without
the hard work of our staff.

We would like to acknowledge:

BENJAMIN BREZNER   *Managing Editor*
MELANIE TAGUE   *Managing Editor*

MARCOS L. MARTINEZ   *Founding Editor*
MEGHAN McNAMARA   *Media & Marketing Advisor*
MICHELLE WEBBER   *Communications/Marketing Director*
SCOTT W. BERG   *Editorial Advisor*
HANNAH CAMPEANEAU   *Editorial Assistant*
HAILEY SCHERER   *Editorial Intern*
CAROLINE HOLMES   *Editorial Intern*

ANONYMOUS   *Our Donors*
THERESE HOWELL
DALLLAS HUDGENS
WAYNE B. JOHNSON
WILLIAM MILLER

STILL
HOUSE
PRESS

CHRISTINA OLSON

is the author of the collection *Before I Came Home Naked* and the chapbooks *Weird Science* and *Rook & The M.E.: A Law & Order-Inspired Narrative*. Her poetry and nonfiction has appeared in *Arts & Letters*, *Virginia Quarterly Review*, *The Southern Review*, *Brevity*, *River Styx*, *Gulf Coast*, *Passages North*, *The Normal School*, *Hayden's Ferry Review*, and *The Best Creative Nonfiction, Volume 3*. She teaches creative writing at Georgia Southern University. Her web site is www.thedrevlow-olsonshow.com.

CPSIA information can be obtained
at www.ICGtesting.com
Printed in the USA
FSHW022113240220
67354FS